# Second Book of Trombone Solos

*Zweites Spielbuch für Posaune und Klavier*

edited and arranged for trombone/euphonium and piano by
*herausgegeben und bearbeitet für Posaune/Euphonium und Klavier von*

## PETER GOODWIN
and
## LESLIE PEARSON

**FABER MUSIC**

# *Contents : Inhalt*


Page/Seite

AB TROM G4 1 Hail Columbia *Gottschalk* 2

2 End Titles *Pearson* 2

3 Intermezzo *Brahms* 3

AB TROM G4 4 Sonata *Fontana* 3

5 Les Deux Robinets *Ravel* 4

6 Salon Waltz *Musorgsky* 4

7 Aria *Pergolesi* 6

8 Nessun Dorma *Puccini* 7

9 Minuet *de Fesch* 8

10 Allegro from Sonata No. 1 *Marcello* 8

11 Presto from Sonata No. 1 *Gabrielli* 9

AB TROM G5 12 Sonata in F minor *Telemann* 10

13 Irish Tune *Grainger* 10

AB TROM G6 14 Song of the Comptois Clock *Ravel* 11




First published in 1989 by Faber Music Ltd
3 Queen Square London WC1N 3AU
Cover design by Roslav Szaybo and Studio Gerrard
Printed in England

# Preface

*Second Book of Trombone Solos* is for the player who already has a reasonably well developed technique and range but is not yet ready for the sonata and concerto repertoire. Like *First Book of Trombone Solos* the pieces are arranged in order of increasing difficulty and are equivalent to Associated Board (U.K.) Grade 4 upwards.

We have endeavoured to choose a wide range of composers, periods and musical styles. We hope you will enjoy playing the pieces in this book and that the opportunity to work with a pianist will not only improve your trombone technique but also help you develop as a mature musician.

The notes on technique and performance at the end of the book should be taken as hints and suggestions, not instructions!

PETER GOODWIN
LESLIE PEARSON

# Vorwort

*Zweites Spielbuch für Posaune und Klavier* ist für den Spieler geeignet, dessen Technik und Tonumfang schon relativ weit entwickelt ist, der aber noch nicht für das Sonaten- und Konzertrepertoire bereit ist. Wie im *Ersten Spielbuch für Posaune und Klavier* sind die Stücke angeordnet nach zunehmendem Schwierigkeitsgrad, und eignen sich für Spieler mit mindestens zwei Jahren Praxis.

Wir haben uns bemüht, einen weiten Bereich an Komponisten, Zeitaltern und musikalischen Stilen auszuwählen. Wir hoffen, daß es Spaß macht, die Stücke in diesem Buch zu spielen und daß die Gelegenheit, mit Pianobegleitung zu spielen, nicht nur Deine Posaunentechnik fördert, sondern Dir auch bei Deiner Entwicklung zu einem reifen Musiker hilft.

Die Anmerkungen zu Technik und Spiel am Ende des Buches sollten als Hinweise und Vorschläge und nicht als Instruktionen angesehen werden!

PETER GOODWIN
LESLIE PEARSON

# 1. HAIL COLUMBIA

Louis Moreau Gottschalk
(1829–1869)

# 2. END TITLES

Leslie Pearson
(1931–    )

6

# 3. INTERMEZZO

Johannes Brahms
(1833–1897)

# 4. SONATA

Giovanni Battista Fontana
(d. 1630)

# 5. LES DEUX ROBINETS

Maurice Ravel
(1875–1937)

# 6. SALON WALTZ

*Salonwalzer*

Modest Petrovich Musorgsky
(1839–1881)

# 7. ARIA
*Arie*

Giovanni Pergolesi
(1710–1736)

# 8. NESSUN DORMA

Giacomo Puccini
(1858–1924)

# 9. MINUET
*Menuett*

Willem de Fesch
(1687–1761)

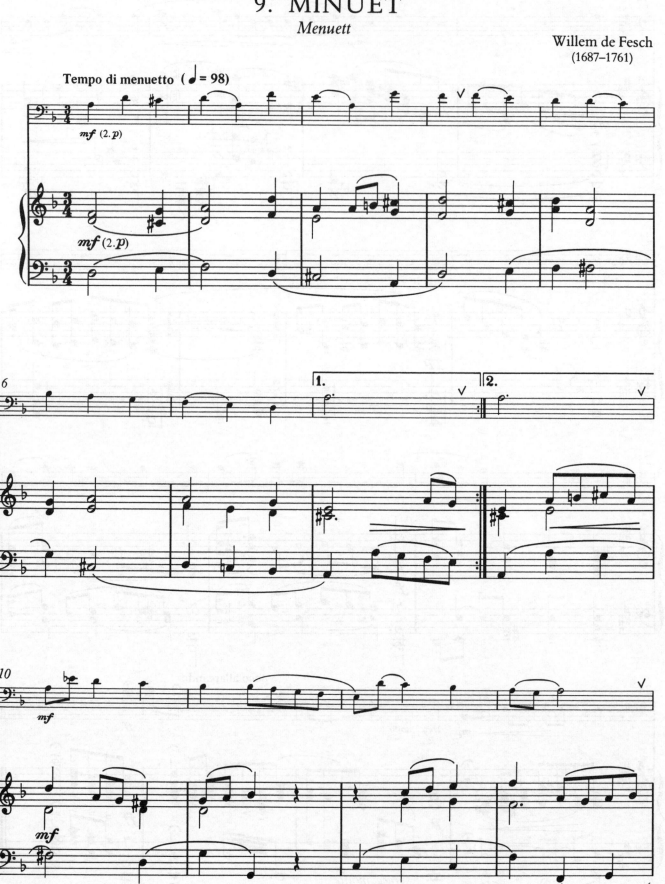

# Second Book of Trombone Solos

*Zweites Spielbuch für
Posaune und Klavier*

edited and arranged for trombone/euphonium and piano by
*herausgegeben und bearbeitet für Posaune/Euphonium und Klavier von*

## PETER GOODWIN
and
## LESLIE PEARSON

FABER MUSIC

2

# 1. HAIL COLUMBIA

Louis Moreau Gottschalk
(1829–1869)

# 2. END TITLES

Leslie Pearson
(1931–    )

## 3. INTERMEZZO

Johannes Brahms
(1833–1897)

## 4. SONATA

Giovanni Battista Fontana
(d. 1630)

**4**

# 5. LES DEUX ROBINETS

Maurice Ravel
(1875–1937)

# 6. SALON WALTZ

*Salonwalzer*

Modest Petrovich Musorgsky
(1839–1881)

# 7. ARIA
*Arie*

Giovanni Pergolesi
(1710–1736)

# 8. NESSUN DORMA

Giacomo Puccini
(1858–1924)

# 9. MINUET
## *Menuett*

Willem de Fesch
(1687–1761)

# 10. ALLEGRO FROM SONATA NO. 1
## *Allegro aus der Sonate Nr. 1*

Benedetto Marcello
(1686–1739)

# 11. PRESTO FROM SONATA NO. 1

*Presto aus der Sonate Nr. 1*

Domenico Gabrielli
(1659–1690)

# 12. SONATA IN F MINOR

*Sonate in F-Moll*

Georg Philipp Telemann
(1681–1767)

# 13. IRISH TUNE

*Irische Melodie*

Percy Grainger
(1882–1961)

# 14.  SONG OF THE COMPTOIS CLOCK

*Lied der Comptois Uhr*

Maurice Ravel
(1875–1937)

# 1. HAIL COLUMBIA

Louis Moreau Gottschalk
(1829–1869)

# 2. END TITLES

Leslie Pearson
(1931–     )

# 5. LES DEUX ROBINETS

Maurice Ravel
(1875–1937)

# 6. SALON WALTZ

*Salonwalzer*

Modest Petrovich Musorgsky
(1839–1881)

# 7. ARIA
*Arie*

Giovanni Pergolesi
(1710–1736)

## 8. NESSUN DORMA

Giacomo Puccini
(1858–1924)

18

# 9. MINUET
*Menuett*

Willem de Fesch
(1687–1761)

# 10. ALLEGRO FROM SONATA NO. 1
*Allegro aus der Sonate Nr. 1*

Benedetto Marcello
(1686–1739)

## 11. PRESTO FROM SONATA NO. 1

*Presto aus der Sonate Nr. 1*

Domenico Gabrielli
(1659–1690)

# 12. SONATA IN F MINOR

*Sonate in F-Moll*

Georg Philipp Telemann
(1681–1767)

# 13. IRISH TUNE

*Irische Melodie*

Percy Grainger
(1882–1961)

# 14. SONG OF THE COMPTOIS CLOCK

*Lied der Comptois Uhr*

Maurice Ravel
(1875–1937)

# NOTES

1. The American pianist and composer Louis Gottschalk was born in New Orleans in 1829. Gottschalk's pieces, mainly for piano, reflect the Negro spiritual and early jazz influences of his birthplace. This song arrangement should sound quite patriotic. To achieve the *Maestoso* (majestic) atmosphere you should make sure that the dotted quaver-semiquaver rhythms are played accurately, particularly when they follow triplets as in bar 12.

2. 'End Title' is the name given to the music played during the credits at the end of a film. This tuneful piece should be played with some subtlety; for example, make sure you play bars 5 and 6 in a different way from the identical phrase that precedes them. Take care to control the sound quality and intonation on the last seven bars and see if you can make the last note gradually fade away to nothing.

3. This is a movement from a piano Fantasia written in 1892. It should be played *espressivo* (expressively) with a little *rubato* (freely) which should give it a Hungarian feel. The quavers at the beginning of each bar should be played slightly separated and strictly in time, in order to fit with the triplet in the piano accompaniment.

4. Giovanni Fontana was a contemporary of Monteverdi. This Sonata was published in Venice in 1641 and was written for either violin or cornett. Intonation around high F, E♮ and E♭ can be problematic. On most trombones this fifth harmonic tends to be sharp, so take care! The piece should be played strictly in tempo. Phrase markings and dynamics are editorial additions.

5. This short piece comes from Ravel's opera *L'enfant et les sortilèges*. It should be played strictly in tempo. The consecutive quavers should be articulated gently with a soft tongue.

6. Like most Russian composers Musorgsky had to earn his living outside music. He was a civil servant but still found time to write a great deal of music, much of which was later completely re-orchestrated and structurally altered by Rimsky-Korsakov. This waltz comes from *Sorochintsy Fair*, a comic opera based on a story by Gogol. The dance-like rhythms should remain constant throughout. Make sure that the dotted crotchet and quaver are played accurately without a break between them. In the 14-bar section, starting at bar 29, make a smooth transition between the two notes and don't come in late after the crotchet rest!

7. The Neapolitan composer Pergolesi became *maestro di cappella* to the Viceroy of Naples, for whom he worked until his death in 1736 at the age of only 26. This area comes from his opera *La serva padrona*. It is Mozartian in style and should be played in a light and playful manner. Make sure the low B natural is flat enough.

8. Although this famous aria from *Turandot* looks fairly simple, it needs a great deal of musicianship to render Puccini's intentions faithfully. The dynamic range should be highly contrasted and it should be played with the kind of traditional *rubato* used by a great tenor like Placido Domingo.

9. The 18th-century Dutch composer Willem de Fesch seems to have been something of a delinquent. In 1731 he was forced to resign his position as *Kapelmeester* at Antwerp Cathedral because of quarrels with the Chapter and Chapel for which his 'temperamental, mean and slovenly character' was to blame. This minuet gives no hint of his difficult personality. It should be played in a poised and elegant manner with the dance quality consistent throughout. The 9-bar phrase starting at bar 12 should be a little more *cantabile* (singing) in style.

10. Benedetto Marcello was the younger of two musical brothers born in Venice in the 1680s. This sonata comes from a set of six for cello and continuo. It should be played strictly in tempo. The biggest problem for trombonists is breathing, so it is important to take as much breath as possible, particularly before long phrases. Take special care to tune the last note; most players realize that high G is in a sharper position than the usual second, but it is very easy to overdo it.

11. So far as we know, Domenico Gabrielli was not related to the more famous Andrea and Giovanni. His short life (39 years) began and ended in Bologna, although like his namesakes he studied and worked in Venice, where he became organist of San Petronio in 1680. This piece should be played strictly in time and quite briskly. Danger spots for getting behind are bars 12–13 and 20–21. Make only a slight *ritenuto* (holding back) in the penultimate bar. The tenor clef is introduced in this piece. If you are not familiar with it work at bars 18–19 slowly.

12. The prolific German composer Georg Philipp Telemann died in Hamburg in 1767 at the ripe old age of 86. This movement, from one of six sonatas for cello and continuo, was published in Frankfurt in 1715. The tempo marking (*triste* = sadly) indicates a slow speed. Make sure that bars 1 and 2, and thereafter where triplet quavers follow a duplet quaver, are played accurately and give the notes their full value, particularly at the ends of phrases (e.g. bars 5 and 6).

13. The Australian pianist and composer Percy Grainger settled in London in 1901 and made his living as a concert pianist. He was fascinated by the wealth of British folksongs passed down from generation to generation and in 1906 he introduced the use of the wax cylinder phonograph in order to collect and transcribe these songs. This one comes from County Down. E major is a warm key but difficult for intonation on the trombone because of fifth position. You should adopt a very *cantabile* and *rubato* style in order to recreate the expressive way it would be sung in its original unaccompanied form.

14. Like *Les Deux Robinets*, this piece comes from *L'enfant et les sortilèges*. The opera is about an ill-natured and aggressive child who is confined to his room for a misdemeanour. There he is visited by a series of inanimate objects which come to life to berate him for his past mistreatment of them. This piece should be played very quickly (Ravel suggests ♩ = 168) and strictly in tempo. Bars 16, 17 and 18 and the subsequent 22-bar melodic section beginning at bar 21 should have the feeling of 2-in-a-bar.

# ANMERKUNGEN

1. Der amerikanische Pianist und Komponist Louis Gottschalk wurde 1829 in New Orleans geboren. Gottschalks Stücke, hauptsächlich für Klavier geschrieben, spiegeln Einflüsse des Negerspirituals und des frühen Jazz seines Geburtsortes wieder. Diese Liedbearbeitung sollte ziemlich patriotisch klingen. Um die *Maestoso* (die majestätische) Atmosphäre zu erreichen, ist es notwendig, die punktierten Achtel-Sechzehntelrhythmen exakt zu spielen, besonders, wenn ihnen wie in Takt 12 Triolen folgen.

2. 'End Title' wird die Musik genannt, die am Ende eines Films gespielt wird, während die Danksagungen gezeigt werden. Dieses melodische Stück muß mit einigem Feingefühl gespielt werden; es sollte vor allem darauf geachtete werden, daß die Takte 5 und 6 anders gespielt werden als die gleiche Phrase vorher. Achte darauf, daß Tonqualität und Tonansatz der letzten sieben Takte zurückhaltend sind und die letzte Note ganz allmählich verklingt.

3. Dieses ist ein Satz aus der Klavierfantasie aus dem Jahre 1892. Er sollte *espressivo* und mit ein wenig *rubato* (frei) gespielt werden, um ihm einen ungarischen Klang zu geben. Die Achtel am Anfang eines jeden Taktes sollten leicht getrennt und mit exakter Zeiteinhaltung gespielt werden, um zu den Triolen der Klavierbegleitung zu passen.

4. Giovanni Fontana war ein Zeitgenosse Monteverdis. Diese Sonate wurde 1641 in Venedig veröffentlicht und wurde entweder für Geige oder Kornett geschrieben. Die Intonation um das hohe F, E♮ and E♭ herum kann Probleme mit sich bringen. Auf den meisten Posaunen neigt der fünfte Oberton dazu, etwas höher zu sein, es ist darum Vorsicht geboten! Das Stück sollte in exaktem Rhythmus, unter genauer Zeiteinhaltung gespielt werden. Satz- und Dynamikanweisungen sind Ergänzungen des Herausgebers.

5. Dieses kurze Stück stammt aus Ravels Oper *L'enfant et les sortilèges* (Das Kind und die Zaubereien). Es sollte unter genauer Zeiteinhaltung gespielt werden. Die aufeinander folgenden Achtel müssen sanft, mit weicher Zunge hervorgebracht werden.

6. Wie die meisten russischen Komponisten mußte Musorgsky seinen Lebensunterhalt außerhalb der Musik verdienen. Er war Beamter, fand aber dennoch die Zeit, eine große Menge Musik zu schreiben, von der vieles später von Rimsky-Korsakov völlig uminstrumentiert und strukturell verändert wurde. Dieser Walzer kommt aus dem *Sorochintsy Fair* (Der Markt von Sorochintsy), einer Komischen Oper, die auf einer Geschichte Gogols basiert. Die tanzähnlichen Rhythmen sollten durchweg gleichmäßig gehalten werden. Die punktierten Viertel und Achtel werden exakt und ohne Bruch gespielt. In dem 14-Takte-Teil, beginnend mit Takt 29, muß ein gleitender Übergang zwischen den beiden Noten erreicht werden, wobei der Einsatz nach der Viertelpause nicht verspätet sein sollte!

7. Der neapolitanische Komponist Pergolesi wurde *maestro di capella* (Kapellmeister) des Vizekönigs von Neapel, für den er bis 1736, bis zu seinem Tode im Alter von nur 26 Jahren arbeitete. Diese Arie stammt aus seiner Oper *La serva padrona*. Sie ist von mozartartigem Stil und sollte leicht und spielerisch geblasen werden. Vorsicht, daß das tiefe B mit aufgelöstem Vorzeichen genau getroffen wird.

8. Obwohl diese berühmte Arie aus *Turandot* verhältnismäßig leicht aussieht, bedarf es eines großen Maßes an Musikerkönnen, Puccinis Vorhaben getreulich zu treffen. Der Dynamikbereich sollte stark konstrastierend und das Spiel mit einer Art von traditionellem *rubato* erfolgen, wie es von einem großen Tenor wie Placido Domingo angewandt wird.

9. Der holländische Komponist des 18. Jahrhunderts Willem de Fesch scheint eine Art von Missetäter gewesen zu sein. Im Jahre 1731 wurde er gezwungen seine Stellung als *Kapellmeister* des Domes von Antwerpen wegen einer Auseinandersetzung mit dem Kapitel der Kapelle aufzugeben, wofür sein 'aufbrausender, gemeiner und unordentlicher Charakter' verantwortlich zu machen war. Dieses Menuett bietet keinerlei Hinweis auf seine schwierige Perönlichkeit. Es sollte in gesetzter, eleganter Weise gespielt werden, mit durchgehendem Tanzcharakter. Der 9-Takte-Satz, beginnend bei Takt 12, sollte vom Stil her etwas mehr *cantabile* (singend) sein.

10. Benedetto Marcello war der jüngere von zwei musikalischen Brüdern, die in den 1680er Jahren in Venedig geboren wurden. Dieses ist eine Sonate aus einem Satz von insgesamt sechs für Cello und Continuo. Sie sollte mit genau eingehaltenem Tempo gespielt werden. Das größte Problem für Posaunenbläser ist die Atmung, und aus diesem Grunde ist es wichtig, so viel Atem wie möglich zu holen, ganz besonders vor langen Phrasen. Bis zur letzten Note sollte besondere Vorsicht beim Anstimmen walten; den meisten Bläsern ist es klar, daß sich das hohe G auf einer höheren Lagenposition befindet als das normale zweite, aber es ist auch möglich, dies zu übertreiben.

11. Soweit es uns bekannt ist, war Domenico Gabrielli nicht mit den bekannteren Andrea und Giovanni verwandt. Sein kurzes Leben (39 Jahre) begann und endete in Bologna, obwohl er wie seine Namensvetter in Venedig studierte und arbeitete, wo er 1680 Organist von San Petronio wurde. Dieses Stück sollte mit exakter Zeiteinhaltung und ziemlich flott gespielt werden. Die Stellen, an denen die Gefahr besteht, daß man zu langsam wird, sind die Takte 12 – 13 und 20 – 21. Blase nur ein ganz geringes *ritenuto* (Verhalten) im vorletzten Takt. Der Tenorschlüssel ist in diesem Stück eingeführt worden. Falls dies ungewohnt ist, zunächst langsam die Takte 18–19 üben.

12. Der produktive deutsche Komponist Georg Philipp Telemann starb 1767 in Hamburg im hohen Alter von 86 Jahren. Dieser Satz, einer von sechs Sonaten für Cello und Continuo, wurde 1715 in Frankfurt veröffentlicht. Die Zeitmarkierungen (*triste* =traurig) weisen ein langsames Tempo an. Es ist darauf zu achten, daß die Takte 1 und 2 und danach, die Stellen, wo Achteltriolen einer Doppelachtelnote folgen, exakt gespielt und die Noten voll ausgehalten werden, insbesondere am Ende der Phrasen (z.B. Takt 5 und 6).

Der australische Pianist und Komponist Percy Grainger ließ sich 1901 in London nieder und verdiente seinen Lebensunterhalt als Konzertpianist. Er war fasziniert von dem Reichtum an britischen Volksliedern, die von Generation zu Generation weitergegeben worden waren, und im Jahre 1906 begann er als erster, diese Lieder mit Hilfe des Wachszylinder-Phonographen zu sammeln und aufzuzeichnen. Dieses hier kommt aus der Grafschaft Down. E-Dur ist eine warme Tonart, aber schwer auf der Posaune zu intonieren aufgrund der fünften Lage. Ein ausgeprägter *cantabile* und *rubato*-Stil sollte angenommen werden, um die ausdrucksvolle Art zu treffen, wie es der ursprünglich unbegleiteten Gesangsform entspricht.

14. Wie *Les Deux Robinets*, stammt dieses Stück ebenfalls aus *L'enfant et les sortilèges*. Die Oper handelt von einem boshaften und aggressiven Kind, das wegen seines Mißverhaltens in sein Zimmer eingesperrt wurde. Dort wird es von einer Reihe lebloser Objekte besucht, die zum Leben erstehen, um es für alle früheren Mißhandlungen auszuschelten. Dieses Stück sollte sehr schnell (Ravel schlägt =168 vor) und mit genauer Zeiteinhaltung gespielt werden. Die Takte 16, 17 und 18 und die darauf folgende 22-Takte-Sektion, beginnend bei Takt 21, sollte in einem 2-pro-Takt-Gefühl gespielt werde.

Deutsche Übersetzung: Helga Braun

# 10.  ALLEGRO FROM SONATA NO. 1

*Allegro aus der Sonate Nr. 1*

Benedetto Marcello
(1686–1739)

# 11. PRESTO FROM SONATA NO. 1

*Presto aus der Sonate Nr. 1*

Domenico Gabrielli
(1659–1690)

# 12. SONATA IN F MINOR

*Sonate in F-Moll*

Georg Philipp Telemann
(1681–1767)

# 13. IRISH TUNE

*Irische Melodie*

Percy Grainger
(1882–1961)

# 14. SONG OF THE COMPTOIS CLOCK

*Lied der Comptois Uhr*

Maurice Ravel
(1875–1937)

Reproduced and printed by
Halstan & Co. Ltd., Amersham, Bucks., England

# NOTES

1. The American pianist and composer Louis Gottschalk was born in New Orleans in 1829. Gottschalk's pieces, mainly for piano, reflect the Negro spiritual and early jazz influences of his birthplace. This song arrangement should sound quite patriotic. To achieve the *Maestoso* (majestic) atmosphere you should make sure that the dotted quaver-semiquaver rhythms are played accurately, particularly when they follow triplets as in bar 12.

2. 'End Title' is the name given to the music played during the credits at the end of a film. This tuneful piece should be played with some subtlety; for example, make sure you play bars 5 and 6 in a different way from the identical phrase that precedes them. Take care to control the sound quality and intonation on the last seven bars and see if you can make the last note gradually fade away to nothing.

3. This is a movement from a piano Fantasia written in 1892. It should be played *espressivo* (expressively) with a little *rubato* (freely) which should give it a Hungarian feel. The quavers at the beginning of each bar should be played slightly separated and strictly in time, in order to fit with the triplet in the piano accompaniment.

4. Giovanni Fontana was a contemporary of Monteverdi. This Sonata was published in Venice in 1641 and was written for either violin or cornett. Intonation around high F, E♮ and E♭ can be problematic. On most trombones this fifth harmonic tends to be sharp, so take care! The piece should be played strictly in tempo. Phrase markings and dynamics are editorial additions.

5. This short piece comes from Ravel's opera *L'enfant et les sortilèges*. It should be played strictly in tempo. The consecutive quavers should be articulated gently with a soft tongue.

6. Like most Russian composers Musorgsky had to earn his living outside music. He was a civil servant but still found time to write a great deal of music, much of which was later completely re-orchestrated and structurally altered by Rimsky-Korsakov. This waltz comes from *Sorochintsy Fair*, a comic opera based on a story by Gogol. The dance-like rhythms should remain constant throughout. Make sure that the dotted crotchet and quaver are played accurately without a break between them. In the 14-bar section, starting at bar 29, make a smooth transition between the two notes and don't come in late after the crotchet rest!

7. The Neapolitan composer Pergolesi became *maestro di cappella* to the Viceroy of Naples, for whom he worked until his death in 1736 at the age of only 26. This area comes from his opera *La serva padrona*. It is Mozartian in style and should be played in a light and playful manner. Make sure the low B natural is flat enough.

8. Although this famous aria from *Turandot* looks fairly simple, it needs a great deal of musicianship to render Puccini's intentions faithfully. The dynamic range should be highly contrasted and it should be played with the kind of traditional *rubato* used by a great tenor like Placido Domingo.

9. The 18th-century Dutch composer Willem de Fesch seems to have been something of a delinquent. In 1731 he was forced to resign his position as *Kapelmeester* at Antwerp Cathedral because of quarrels with the Chapter and Chapel for which his 'temperamental, mean and slovenly character' was to blame. This minuet gives no hint of his difficult personality. It should be played in a poised and elegant manner with the dance quality consistent thoughout. The 9-bar phrase starting at bar 12 should be a little more *cantabile* (singing) in style.

10. Benedetto Marcello was the younger of two musical brothers born in Venice in the 1680s. This sonata comes from a set of six for cello and continuo. It should be played strictly in tempo. The biggest problem for trombonists is breathing, so it is important to take as much breath as possible, particularly before long phrases. Take special care to tune the last note; most players realize that high G is in a sharper position than the usual second, but it is very easy to overdo it.

11. So far as we know, Domenico Gabrielli was not related to the more famous Andrea and Giovanni. His short life (39 years) began and ended in Bologna, although like his namesakes he studied and worked in Venice, where he became organist of San Petronio in 1680. This piece should be played strictly in time and quite briskly. Danger spots for getting behind are bars 12–13 and 20–21. Make only a slight *ritenuto* (holding back) in the penultimate bar. The tenor clef is introduced in this piece. If you are not familiar with it work at bars 18–19 slowly.

12. The prolific German composer Georg Philipp Telemann died in Hamburg in 1767 at the ripe old age of 86. This movement, from one of six sonatas for cello and continuo, was published in Frankfurt in 1715. The tempo marking (*triste* = sadly) indicates a slow speed. Make sure that bars 1 and 2, and thereafter where triplet quavers follow a duplet quaver, are played accurately and give the notes their full value, particularly at the ends of phrases (e.g. bars 5 and 6).

13. The Australian pianist and composer Percy Grainger settled in London in 1901 and made his living as a concert pianist. He was fascinated by the wealth of British folksongs passed down from generation to generation and in 1906 he introduced the use of the wax cylinder phonograph in order to collect and transcribe these songs. This one comes from County Down. E major is a warm key but difficult for intonation on the trombone because of fifth position. You should adopt a very *cantabile* and *rubato* style in order to recreate the expressive way it would be sung in its original unaccompanied form.

14. Like *Les Deux Robinets*, this piece comes from *L'enfant et les sortilèges*. The opera is about an ill-natured and aggressive child who is confined to his room for a misdemeanour. There he is visited by a series of inanimate objects which come to life to berate him for his past mistreatment of them. This piece should be played very quickly (Ravel suggests ♩ = 168) and strictly in tempo. Bars 16, 17 and 18 and the subsequent 22-bar melodic section beginning at bar 21 should have the feeling of 2-in-a-bar.

# ANMERKUNGEN

1. Der amerikanische Pianist und Komponist Louis Gottschalk wurde 1829 in New Orleans geboren. Gottschalks Stücke, hauptsächlich für Klavier geschrieben, spiegeln Einflüsse des Negerspirituals und des frühen Jazz seines Geburtsortes wieder. Diese Liedbearbeitung sollte ziemlich patriotisch klingen. Um die *Maestoso* (die majestätische) Atmosphäre zu erreichen, ist es notwendig, die punktierten Achtel-Sechzehntelrhythmen exakt zu spielen, besonders, wenn ihnen wie in Takt 12 Triolen folgen.

2. 'End Title' wird die Musik genannt, die am Ende eines Films gespielt wird, während die Danksagungen gezeigt werden. Dieses melodische Stück muß mit einigem Feingefühl gespielt werden; es sollte vor allem darauf geachtete werden, daß die Takte 5 und 6 anders gespielt werden als dic gleiche Phrase vorher. Achte darauf, daß Tonqualität und Tonansatz der letzten sieben Takte zurückhaltend sind und die letzte Note ganz allmählich verklingt.

3. Dieses ist ein Satz aus der Klavierfantasie aus dem Jahre 1892. Er sollte *espressivo* und mit ein wenig *rubato* (frei) gespielt werden, um ihm einen ungarischen Klang zu geben. Die Achtel am Anfang eines jeden Taktes sollten leicht getrennt und mit exakter Zeiteinhaltung gespielt werden, um zu den Triolen der Klavierbegleitung zu passen.

4. Giovanni Fontana war ein Zeitgenosse Monteverdis. Diese Sonate wurde 1641 in Venedig veröffentlicht und wurde entweder für Geige oder Kornett geschrieben. Die Intonation um das hohe F, E♮ and E♭ herum kann Probleme mit sich bringen. Auf den meisten Posaunen neigt der fünfte Oberton dazu, etwas höher zu sein, es ist darum Vorsicht geboten! Das Stück sollte in exaktem Rhythmus, unter genauer Zeiteinhaltung gespielt werden. Satz- und Dynamikanweisungen sind Ergänzungen des Herausgebers.

5. Dieses kurze Stück stammt aus Ravels Oper *L'enfant et les sortilèges* (Das Kind und die Zaubereien). Es sollte unter genauer Zeiteinhaltung gespielt werden. Die aufeinander folgenden Achtel müssen sanft, mit weicher Zunge hervorgebracht werden.

6. Wie die meisten russischen Komponisten mußte Musorgsky seinen Lebensunterhalt außerhalb der Musik verdienen. Er war Beamter, fand aber dennoch die Zeit, eine große Menge Musik zu schreiben, von der vieles später von Rimsky-Korsakov völlig uminstrumentiert und strukturell verändert wurde. Dieser Walzer kommt aus dem *Sorochintsy Fair* (Der Markt von Sorochintsy), einer Komischen Oper, die auf einer Geschichte Gogols basiert. Die tanzähnlichen Rhythmen sollten durchweg gleichmäßig gehalten werden. Die punktierten Viertel und Achtel werden exakt und ohne Bruch gespielt. In dem 14-Takte-Teil, beginnend mit Takt 29, muß ein gleitender Übergang zwischen den beiden Noten erreicht werden, wobei der Einsatz nach der Viertelpause nicht verspätet sein sollte!

7. Der neapolitanische Komponist Pergolesi wurde *maestro di capella* (Kapellmeister) des Vizekönigs von Neapel, für den er bis 1736, bis zu seinem Tode im Alter von nur 26 Jahren arbeitete. Diese Arie stammt aus seiner Oper *La serva padrona*. Sie ist von mozartartigem Stil und sollte leicht und spielerisch geblasen werden. Vorsicht, daß das tiefe B mit aufgelöstem Vorzeichen genau getroffen wird.

8. Obwohl diese berühmte Arie aus *Turandot* verhältnismäßig leicht aussieht, bedarf es eines großen Maßes an Musikerkönnen, Puccinis Vorhaben getreulich zu treffen. Der Dynamikbereich sollte stark konstrastierend und das Spiel mit einer Art von traditionellem *rubato* erfolgen, wie es von einem großen Tenor wie Placido Domingo angewandt wird.

9. Der holländische Komponist des 18. Jahrhunderts Willem de Fesch scheint eine Art von Missetäter gewesen zu sein. Im Jahre 1731 wurde er gezwungen seine Stellung als *Kapellmeister* des Domes von Antwerpen wegen einer Auseinandersetzung mit dem Kapitel der Kapelle aufzugeben, wofür sein 'aufbrausender, gemeiner und unordentlicher Charakter' verantwortlich zu machen war. Dieses Menuett bietet keinerlei Hinweis auf seine schwierige Perönlichkeit. Es sollte in gesetzter, eleganter Weise gespielt werden, mit durchgehendem Tanzcharakter. Der 9-Takte-Satz, beginnend bei Takt 12, sollte vom Stil her etwas mehr *cantabile* (singend) sein.

10. Benedetto Marcello war der jüngere von zwei musikalischen Brüdern, die in den 1680er Jahren in Venedig geboren wurden. Dieses ist eine Sonate aus einem Satz von insgesamt sechs für Cello und Continuo. Sie sollte mit genau eingehaltenem Tempo gespielt werden. Das größte Problem für Posaunenbläser ist die Atmung, und aus diesem Grunde ist es wichtig, so viel Atem wie möglich zu holen, ganz besonders vor langen Phrasen. Bis zur letzten Note sollte besondere Vorsicht beim Anstimmen walten; den meisten Bläsern ist es klar, daß sich das hohe G auf einer höheren Lagenposition befindet als das normale zweite, aber es ist auch möglich, dies zu übertreiben.

11. Soweit es uns bekannt ist, war Domenico Gabrielli nicht mit den bekannteren Andrea und Giovanni verwandt. Sein kurzes Leben (39 Jahre) begann und endete in Bologna, obwohl er wie seine Namensvettern in Venedig studierte und arbeitete, wo er 1680 Organist von San Petronio wurde. Dieses Stück sollte mit exakter Zeiteinhaltung und ziemlich flott gespielt werden. Die Stellen, an denen die Gefahr besteht, daß man zu langsam wird, sind die Takte 12 – 13 und 20 – 21. Blase nur ein ganz geringes *ritenuto* (Verhalten) im vorletzten Takt. Der Tenorschlüssel ist in diesem Stück eingeführt worden. Falls dies ungewohnt ist, zunächst langsam die Takte 18–19 üben.

12. Der produktive deutsche Komponist Georg Philipp Telemann starb 1767 in Hamburg im hohen Alter von 86 Jahren. Dieser Satz, einer von sechs Sonaten für Cello und Continuo, wurde 1715 in Frankfurt veröffentlicht. Die Zeitmarkierungen (*triste* =traurig) weisen ein langsames Tempo an. Es ist darauf zu achten, daß die Takte 1 und 2 und danach, die Stellen, wo Achteltriolen einer Doppelachtelnote folgen, exakt gespielt und die Noten voll ausgehalten werden, insbesondere am Ende der Phrasen (z.B. Takt 5 und 6).

13. Der australische Pianist und Komponist Percy Grainger ließ sich 1901 in London nieder und verdiente seinen Lebensunterhalt als Konzertpianist. Er war fasziniert von dem Reichtum an britischen Volksliedern, die von Generation zu Generation weitergegeben worden waren, und im Jahre 1906 begann er als erster, diese Lieder mit Hilfe des Wachszylinder-Phonographen zu sammeln und aufzuzeichnen. Dieses hier kommt aus der Grafschaft Down. E-Dur ist eine warme Tonart, aber schwer auf der Posaune zu intonieren aufgrund der fünften Lage. Ein ausgeprägter *cantabile* und *rubato*-Stil sollte angenommen werden, um die ausdrucksvolle Art zu treffen, wie es der ursprünglich unbegleiteten Gesangsform entspricht.

14. Wie *Les Deux Robinets*, stammt dieses Stück ebenfalls aus *L'enfant et les sortilèges*. Die Oper handelt von einem boshaften und aggressiven Kind, das wegen seines Mißverhaltens in sein Zimmer eingesperrt wurde. Dort wird es von einer Reihe lebloser Objekte besucht, die zum Leben erstehen, um es für alle früheren Mißhandlungen auszuschelten. Dieses Stück sollte sehr schnell (Ravel schlägt=168 vor) und mit genauer Zeiteinhaltung gespielt werden. Die Takte 16, 17 und 18 und die darauf folgende 22-Takte-Sektion, beginnend bei Takt 21, sollte in einem 2-pro-Takt-Gefühl gespielt werde.

Deutsche Übersetzung: Helga Braun